Betty Sapson

John Wesley's Little Instruction Book

A Classic Treasury of
Timeless Wisdom and Reflection

D0367582

Tulsa, Oklahoma

John Wesley's Little Instruction Book
A Classic Treasury of Timeless Wisdom and Reflection
ISBN 1-56292-027-8

Copyright © 1996 by Honor Books, Inc.
P. O. Box 55388
Tulsa, Oklahoma 74155

Introduction

The ministry of John Wesley (1709-1791) had an impact on the world that can still be seen today. As an ordained priest in the Church of England, he reacted to the deadness and formalism of his day by evangelizing and preaching holiness, or living the Christian life according to Christ's commands.

Wesley came from a godly lineage on both sides of his family and from an early age sought to live righteously. After many years of spiritual frustration, he surrendered his life to Jesus Christ, and through a relationship with Him finally found freedom from sin and the strength to live a godly life.

Wesley preached holy living thoughout the British Isles, traveling hundreds of thousands of miles on horseback. The believers he left behind had assurance of their salvation and were determined to live for God. Though he defended and stayed within the Church of England, the Christian life he taught, termed "Methodism," spread around the world. Today, Methodist and other Wesleyan denominations comprise a large sect of Protestantism.

The hallmark of John Wesley's ministry was total commitment and surrender of all to God in order for Christ's character to be formed in us. This powerful message is still needed and greatly cherished by believers everywhere.

Note: All quotes are John Wesley unless indicated otherwise.

⌒ BE A "DO GOODER" ⌒

"Do all the good you can,
By all the means you can,
In all the ways you can,
To all the people you can,
As long as ever you can."

DID YOU KNOW?

John Wesley was the fifteenth of eighteen children,
eight of whom died in infancy.

⌒ HIS FATHER'S ⌒ SPIRITUAL LINEAGE

John's father and paternal grandfather (also named John) were Oxford men and preachers. His father wrote several books. His paternal great-grandfather, Bartholomew Wesley, was a Puritan clergyman.

⌒ HIS MOTHER'S ⌒ SPIRITUAL LINEAGE

While yet in her teens Susannah knew Greek, Latin, and French. She had read the Early Fathers and was wrestling with philosophical ideas while other girls were still playing with dolls.

⌒ HIS MOTHER'S ⌒ SPIRITUAL LINEAGE

Susannah inherited her zeal from her father, Dr. Annesley, a well-known Puritan minister. When a friend inquired how many children Dr. Annesley had a friend answered, "I believe it is two dozen or a quarter of a hundred."

DID YOU KNOW?

At seven years old, Wesley almost perished in a fire. After being snatched from the blaze by a neighbor, his mother reminded him that he was "a brand plucked from the burning" for the purpose of serving God.

⁓ THE MYSTERY ⁓ OF ETERNITY

"The mind does not see either the beauties or the terrors of eternity, because they are so distant from us. It is as if they had no existence. Meanwhile, we are wholly taken up with things present till our nature is changed by grace."

STRUGGLING TO DO GOOD...

"In 1730 I began visiting the prisons, assisting the poor and sick in town, and doing what other good I could by my presence or my little fortune to the bodies and souls of all men."

BEFORE CONVERSION

"I had many remarkable returns to prayer, especially when I was in trouble...But I was still under the law, not under grace, for I was only striving with, not freed from, sin."

MISSIONARY?

"It is now two years and almost four months since I left my native country, in order to teach the Georgian Indians the nature of Christianity: But...I who went to America to convert others, was never myself converted to God."

FEAR OF DEATH

"In my return to England, January 1738, being in imminent danger of death and very uneasy on that account, I was strongly convinced that the cause of that uneasiness was unbelief and that gaining a true, living faith was the one thing needful for me."

JESUS IS THE KEY

"But still I fixed not this faith on its right object: I meant only faith in God, not faith in or through Christ."

———————

"I am the way, the truth, and the life: no man cometh unto the Father but by me."

JOHN 14:6

A DESIRE FOR GOD

"O grant that nothing in my soul
May dwell, but Thy *pure love* alone!
O may Thy love *possess me whole.*
"My joy, my treasure, and my crown.
Strange flames far from my heart remove!
My *every* act, word, thought, be love."

UPON HEARING LUTHER'S PREFACE TO THE EPISTLE TO THE ROMANS...

"While he was describing the change which God works in the heart through faith in Christ, I felt my heart strangely warmed."

HE IS CONVERTED

"I felt I did trust in Christ, Christ alone for salvation; and an assurance was given me that he had taken away *my* sins, even *mine*, and saved *me* from the law of sin and death."

AT 35 YEARS OLD...

"By a Christian I mean one who so believes in Christ as that sin hath no more dominion over him; and in this obvious sense of the word I was not a Christian till May the 24th last past [1738]."

"There is therefore now no condemnation to them which are in Christ Jesus, who walk not after the flesh, but after the Spirit."

ROMANS 8:1

A TRUE CHRISTIAN

"For till then sin had the dominion over me, although I fought with it continually; from that time to this it hath not, such is the free grace of God in Christ."

"For the law of the Spirit of life in Christ Jesus hath made me free from the law of sin and death."

ROMANS 8:2

DID YOU KNOW?

Wesley preached an average of twice a
day for a total of over 40,000 sermons.

His habit was to be up and preaching
by 5:00 a.m. in the morning.

⌒ ONE TIMELY BORN ⌒

Patiently God waited until John Wesley's frustration with sin brought him to simple faith and trust in Jesus Christ. God needed a man like Wesley for a particular time and purpose — to exhort believers to live according to the faith in their hearts.

⌐ CONVERSION OF ⌐ CHARLES WESLEY

A friend read the words, *Blessed is the man whose transgression is forgiven, whose sin is covered.* Charles' eyes fell on the verse, *He hath put a new song in my mouth,...* and God's redemptive work was accomplished in his soul.

John records: "Towards ten my brother was brought in triumph by a troop of our friends, and declared, 'I believe.' We sang the hymn with great joy."

SONG OF SALVATION

"Blessed Jesus, meek and mild,
Look upon a little child;
Pity my simplicity,
Suffer me to come to thee."

Charles Wesley
(from *Hymns and Sacred Poems*)

SAVED...

"He who is thus justified, or saved, by faith is indeed born again of the Spirit. *He is a new creature: old things are passed away; all things in him are become new.*

TO PERFECTION

"And as a new-born babe he gladly receives the *sincere milk of the Word, and grows thereby*...from faith to faith, from grace to grace, until at length he comes into *a perfect man, unto the measure of the stature of the fulness of Christ.*"

GOD'S OMNISCIENCE

"If the eye of man discerns things at a small distance, the eye of an eagle at a greater, and the eye of an angel at ten thousand times greater distance, shall not the eye of God see everything through the whole extent of creation?"

GOD'S OMNI-PRESENCE

"True, our narrow understanding but imperfectly comprehends this. But as He created and sustains all things, He is present at all times, in all places."

"I know that thou canst do everything, and that no thought can be withholden from thee."

JOB 42:2

DIVINE PROTECTION

A clergyman, who *repeatedly* opposed Wesley from the pulpit, was seiged with a throat rattle, fell back from the podium, and died the following Sunday.

⌒ GOD TEACHES ⌒ HOLINESS

"When I was at Oxford...I scarce thought it possible for a man to retain the Christian spirit amidst the noise and bustle of the world. *God* taught me better by my own experience."

QUESTIONS...

"Are you humble, teachable, advisable;
or stubborn, self-willed, heady, and high-minded?
Are you obedient to your superiors as to parents?

FOR YOUNG PEOPLE

"Are you diligent in your business,
pursuing your studies with all your strength?
Do you know how to possess your bodies
in sanctification and honor?"

FREE GRACE...

"It was free grace that *formed man of the dust of the ground, and breathed into him a living soul* and stamped on that soul the image of God...

FOR US

"The same free grace continues to us...
For there is nothing we are, or have, or do
which can deserve the least thing at God's hand."

*"But God commandeth his love toward us, in that,
while we were yet sinners, Christ died for us."*

ROMANS 5:8

DID YOU KNOW?

During his ministry John Wesley rode over 250,000 miles
on horseback, a distance equal to ten circuits of the earth.

⌒ DIVINE TARGET ⌒

"I am a creature of a day, passing through life as an arrow through the air...I am a spirit from God, returning to God."

 A MAN OF THE BOOK

"Here [in the Bible] is knowledge enough for me...
Here then I am far from the busy ways of men.
I sit down alone. Only God is here.
In His presence, I open, I read His Book."

TO A PREACHER LIVING BY FAITH

"When I had only blackberries to eat in Cornwall, still God gave me strength to do my work."

"Neither have I gone back from the commandment of his lips; I have esteemed the works of his mouth more than my necessary food."

JOB 23:12

⌇ THE MIGHTY POWER ⌇ OF GOD

"About three in the morning, as we were continuing instant in prayer, the power of God came mightily upon us, insomuch that many cried out for exceeding joy, and many fell to the ground."

⌒ GOD HAS ⌒ NO BOUNDARIES

"I love the rules and ceremonies of the Church. But I see, well-pleased, that our great Lord can work without them."

SERVANT OF LOVE

"For his obedience is in proportion to his love, the source from whence it flows. And therefore loving God with all his heart, he serves him with all his strength."

☙ MARKS OF A CHRISTIAN ❧

"Entirely and without reserve, devoting himself, all he has, all he is, to his glory. All the talents he has, he constantly employs according to his master's will."

A BELIEVER'S CHECKLIST

"Do you always find a clear sense of the presence of the ever-blessed Trinity? Are you enabled to rejoice evermore? Do you pray without ceasing? And can you in everything give thanks?"

⌒ BUSY BUT ⌒ NEVER HURRIED

"Though I am always in haste, I am never in a hurry; because I never undertake any more work than I can go through with perfect calmness of spirit."

DID YOU KNOW?

John Wesley has been called "The Father of the Religious Paperback." Around 5000 items came from his pen — sermons, tracks, and pamplets of every kind.

GAIN WISELY

"We ought not to gain money at the expense of life nor at the expense of our health."

"Do not wear yourself out to get rich; have the wisdom to show restraint."

PROVERBS 23:4 NIV

SPENDING...

"If a doubt should arise in your mind concerning what you should spend on yourself or your family, calmly inquire: (1) In expending this sum, am I acting according to my character? Am I acting as a steward of my Lord's goods?

THE LORD'S MONEY

"(2) Am I doing this in obedience to His Word? (3) Can I offer up this action as a sacrifice to God through Jesus Christ? (4) Have I reason to believe that for this I shall have a reward at the resurrection of the just?"

STAY WITH SCRIPTURE

"It is dangerous to depart from Scripture...most of the controversies which have disturbed the Church have arisen from people's wanting to be wise above what is written, not contented with what God has plainly revealed there."

HIS HOPE

"I have a good hope that you will never lose any of the things which He has wrought in you, but that you will receive a full reward!"

"For I know whom I have believed, and am pursuaded that he is able to keep that which I have committed unto him against that day."

2 TIMOTHY 1:12

⌒ WISE ADVICE ⌒
TO A PREACHER

"If you would not murder yourself, take particular care never to preach too loud or too long. Always conclude the service within the hour. Then preaching will not hurt you."

⌒ TRUTHS UNITING US ⌒

Wesley is described by scholars as one who glimpsed the underlying unity of Christian truth in both the Catholic and Protestant traditions, thus inspiring a great religious reform and renewal.

JOHN AND CHARLES...

Two young men without a name, without friends, without either power or fortune, set out to oppose the world's philosophies and lifestyles with the life-changing power of the Gospel.

TWO MEN WHO CHANGED THE WORLD

They attempted a reformation of everything contrary to justice, mercy, or truth. They were treated by many — both great and small — as mad dogs. History proves otherwise!

HUMILITY AMONG PEERS EVEN AFTER A DISPUTE

 woman asked Wesley, "Do you expect to see dear Mr. Whitefield in heaven?" "No, madam," he answered, "Do not misundertand me. George Whitefield was so bright a star in the fimament of God's glory, and will stand so near the throne, that one like me, who am less than the least, will never catch a glimpse of him."

[George Whitefield, a great revivalist of Wesley's time, ministered extensively in England and the United States.]

HIS SECRETS FOR PRODUCTIVITY

"My constant exercise and change of air. My having sleep at command; so that whenever I feel myself almost worn out, I call it, and it comes, day or night. My having constantly, for above sixty years, risen at four in the morning."

DID YOU KNOW?

Charles was a most gifted and prolific hymnwriter, authoring some 7,270 hymns. Many are found in the hymnals of a variety of denominations.

⌒ BELIEVING THE ⌒ IMPOSSIBLE

"Faith, mighty faith, the promise sees,
And looks to God alone;
Laughs at impossibilities,
And cries, it shall be done."

Charles Wesley

⟜ TENACITY ⟞

Wesley not only stood his ground against violent mobs
who opposed him, but again and again he
returned to the scene later and claimed
it for the kingdom of God.

⟨ WHY DO YOU ⟩
AVOID SIN?

"Good men avoid sin from the love of virtue;
wicked men avoid sin from a fear of punishment."

HEAVEN...

"The inhabitants of heaven continually cry,
"Holy, holy, holy is the Lord, the God, the Almighty,
who was, and who is, and who is to come!"
When millions of ages have elapsed,
their eternity is but just begun...."

AND HELL

"On the other hand, in what condition are those immortal
spirits who have made choice of a miserable eternity...
the lake of fire burning with brimstone,
where they have no rest, day or night.
To be chained there one day or one hour
would seem like a long time."

⪚ THE POWER OF ⪛
THE HOLY SPIRIT

"God has also, through the intercession of His Son, given us His Holy Spirit to renew us both in knowledge and also in His moral image. This being done, we know that *all things work together for our good.*"

⌒ LIVE FOR GOD ⌒

"Be active, be diligent. Avoid all laziness, sloth, indolence. Fly from every degree, every appearance of it; else you will never be more than half a Christian."

⌒ DESTRUCTION ⌒ FROM STRIFE

"How many of these [arguing about religion] have turned their weapons against each other, and so not only wasted their precious time, but hurt one another's spirits, weakened each other's hands, and so hindered the great work of their common Master."

LETTER TO FRANCIS ASBURY

"Let me be nothing,
and 'Christ be all in all.'"

---

*"He must increase,
but I must decrease."*
JOHN 3:30

⤜ THE GREAT ⤛ COMMISSION

"The God of love will then prepare his messengers and make a way into the polar regions, into the deepest recesses of America, and into the interior parts of Africa; yea, into the heart of China and Japan, with the countries adjoining to them. And *their sound* will then *go forth into all lands, and their voice to the ends of the earth.*"

HOLY OPTIMISM

esley's assistant, Samuel Bradburn, said he "never saw him low-spirited in my life, nor could he endure to be with a melancholy person."

DID YOU KNOW?

While students at Oxford University, John and Charles began "The Holy Club," a fellowship of believers which never exceeded twenty-five members.

THE HOLY CLUB

Members fasted, received Holy Communion, studied the Greek New Testament, visited prisoners and the sick, and adhered to a strict code of conduct. Some became bishops, writers, and evangelists, George Whitefield among them.

SILENCING THE OPPOSITION

Twice in one year, Wesley was confronted by howling mobs as he tried to enter his house. Both times he calmly spoke to them about Christ until they listened quietly.

"A soft answer turneth away wrath."

PROVERBS 15:1

⌒ WORDS TO A ⌒ SUFFERING SAINT

"When your warfare is accomplished, when you are made perfect through sufferings, you shall come to your grave, not with sorrow, but as a ripe shock of corn, full of years and victories."

⌒ THE ORIGIN OF ⌒ A FAMOUS SAYING

"Slovenliness is no part of religion. [No] text of Scripture condemns neatness of apparel. Certainly this is a duty, not a sin. *Cleanliness is next to godliness.*"

⌒ A WOMAN DESCRIBES ⌒ HER CONVERSION UNDER WESLEY'S MINISTRY

"And in a moment all things became new. I seemed to have new eyes and a new understanding. I saw all I read in a new light. My burden dropped off. My soul was at peace. My tears were all gone."

AND CAN IT BE

"And can it be that I should gain
An interest in the Savior's blood?
Died he for me, who caused his pain?
For me? Who him to death pursued?
Amazing love! How can it be
That thou, my God, shouldst die for me?"

⌒ AND CAN IT BE ⌒
(v. 2)

"Long my imprisoned spirit lay,
Fast bound in sin and nature's night.
Thine eye diffused a quick'ning ray;
I woke; the dungeon flamed with light.
My chains fell off, my heart was free,
I rose, went forth, and followed thee."

Charles Wesley

The Christian Classics Series

A RIGOROUS ROUTINE

At one point, Wesley called the routine of his ministry "as fixed as the sun." He spent the winters in London and Bristol overseeing the societies, schools, and orphanages. In the summer he was "almost perpetually in motion." He rode throughout England, visited Scotland twenty-two times, and made many journeys to Ireland.

THE PREEMINENCE OF LOVE

"Beware you be not swallowed up in books!
An ounce of love is worth a pound
of knowledge."

⌒ CHANNELS OF LOVE ⌒

"By 'means of grace,' I understand outward signs, words,
or actions, ordained of God and appointed for this end,...
The chief of these means are prayer, whether in secret
or with the great congregation; searching the scriptures,
and receiving the Lord's Supper."

LOVE IS THE GOAL

"You that are yourselves imperfect, know love is your end. All things else are but means. Choose such means as lead you most to love."

DID YOU KNOW?

Benjamin Franklin printed Wesley's sermon,
"On Free Grace."
Wesley read everything Franklin wrote on electricity,
then wrote his own treatise on the subject.
The two men never met.

SPIRITUAL STRENGTH

The secret of Wesley's spirituality lay in his careful and prayerful use of time. His superhuman acheivements were a result of establishing daily habits which kept him focused on God.

His chief gifts, besides being an active preacher, were organization, administration, and writing.

THOUGHTS AT THE END OF THE DAY

"Did I think of God first and last? Have I examined myself, how I behaved since last night's retirement? [Was] I resolved to do all the good I [could] this day, and to be diligent in the business of my calling?"

⌢ THE NEEDS OF OTHERS ⌢

"Make me zealous to embrace all occasions that may administer to their happiness, by assisting the needy, protecting the oppressed, instructing the ignorant, confirming the wavering, exhorting the good, and reproving the wicked."

A PRAYER FOR PURITY

"O my Father, my God, deliver me, I beseech you, from all violent passions: I know how greatly obstructive these are of both the knowledge and the love of you... deliver me, O my God, from all idolatrous self-love. I know the very corruption of the devil is the having of a will contrary to yours."

⟾ A FRESH START ⟾
EVERY SEVEN YEARS

"Once in seven years I burn all my sermons; for it is a shame if I cannot write better sermons now than I did seven years ago."

FALSE HUMILITY

"Beware of that mock humility that pleads as an excuse for willful disobedience, 'O I can do nothing' ...without speaking of grace active in love."

DID YOU KNOW?

Most of the hymns of Charles Wesley were seldom heard in parish churches during his and John's lifetime. They were sung in the market squares and fields of England.

CHRIST THE LORD IS RISEN TODAY

"Christ, the Lord is risen today,
Sons of men and angels say!
Raise your joys and triumphs high:
Sing, ye heaven; thou earth reply."

⌒ CHRIST THE LORD ⌒ IS RISEN TODAY (v. 2)

"Lives again our glorious King!
Where, O death, is now thy sting!
Once he died our souls to save;
Where's thy victory, boasting grave!"

Charles Wesley

A ONCE LEWD...

As Charles Wesley began to sing a hymn at a public service, he was interrupted by a company of half-drunken sailors, singing the indecent song, "Nancy Dawson." A great discord resulted.

SANCTIFIED TUNE

Charles' quick ear mastered the tune and meter of their song. At the very next service, when the sailors were ready to repeat their opposition, he sang a new *hymn* — to the tune of "Nancy Dawson."

DID YOU KNOW?

Handel, who is famous for composing "The Messiah,"
composed tunes expressly for Charles Wesley's hymns.
The musical manuscripts, in Handel's own handwriting,
are preserved at Cambridge University.

RUNNING THE RACE

"If you have stumbled, O seeker of God, do not just lie there fretting and bemoaning your weakness! Patiently pray: 'Lord, I acknowledge that every moment I would be stumbling if you were not upholding me.' And then get up! Leap! Walk! Go on your way! *Run with resolution the race* in which you are entered."

FERVENT PRAYER...

"I am ashamed when I think how long I have lived a stranger, yea, an enemy to thee, taking upon me to dispose of myself, and to please myself in the main course of my life.

OF CONSECRATION

"But now I unfeignedly desire to return unto thee, and renouncing all interest and ownership over myself, give myself up entirely to thee. I would be thine, and only thine for ever. Amen."

ENCOURAGING WILLIAM WILBERFORCE...

"Unless God has raised you up for this very thing,
you will be worn out by the opposition of men and devils.
But if God be for you, who can be against you?"

IN HIS OPPOSITION TO THE SLAVE TRADE

"Go on, in the name of God and in the power of his might, till even American slavery (the vilest that ever saw the sun) shall vanish away before it."

☞ HOLINESS ☜
AND HAPPINESS

"Unless one is born again, one cannot be happy in this world. For it is not possible, in the nature of things, that someone can become truly happy who is not holy."

∼ PRAYER ∼ OF REPENTANCE

"Father, accept my imperfect repentance, be compassionate toward my infirmities, purify my uncleanness, strengthen my weakness, fix my unstableness, and let thy good Spirit watch over me forever, and thy love ever rule in my heart. Amen."

⟿ LIFE'S RULING ⟿ PRINCIPLE

"What is the ruling principle of your life? Is it the love of God? Is it the fear of God? Or is it neither of these, but rather the love of the world, of pleasure, or gain, of ease, of reputation?"

"OUR" WORK

"God works in us, therefore we can work."

———————

"I can do all things through Christ who strengtheneth me."

PHILIPPIANS 4:13

DELAYED REPENTANCE

"We remain quite naive about our own tendencies to self-deception. If we talk loosely of 'repenting by-and-by,' we are careful not to set an exact time."

⌒ FREEDOM FROM SIN ⌒

"To believers in Christ who walk in this way, there is no condemnation for their past sins. God does not condemn their past. It is as though these past sins had never been, as if a stone were thrown to the bottom of the sea."

"It is precisely when sufferings most
abound that the consolation of
God's Spirit abounds."

GOD IS THERE WHEN IT HURTS

"It is expedient for you that
I go away: for if I go not away,
the Comforter will not come
unto you; but if I depart, I will
send him unto you."

JOHN 16:7

JOY IN KNOWING GOD

"...the sons and daughters of God are able in a sense to laugh at violence when it comes — to laugh at economic hardship, pain, hell, and the grave. For they are already acquainted with the One who finally *holds the keys of Death and Death's domain.*"

⮜ DEFINITION ⮞
OF HOLINESS

"By holiness I mean not fasting...or bodily austerity, or any other external means of improvement, but the inward temper, to which all these are subservient, a renewal of the soul in the image of God...a complex habit of lowliness, meekness, purity, faith, hope, and the love of God and man."

DID YOU KNOW?

Wesley had a strong gift as a leader and organizer.
His influence over his followers was so great, one
historian declared he could have led a revolution if
he had not been so wedded to the existing government.

SIGNS...

"Immediately the power of God fell upon us: one, and another, and another sunk to the earth; you might see them dropping on all sides as thunder-struck. One cried out aloud. I went and prayed over her, and she received joy in the Holy Ghost.

OF REVIVAL

"In the evening I made the same appeal to God, and almost before we called He answered. A young woman was seized with such pangs as I never saw before; and in a quarter of an hour she had a new song in her mouth, a thanksgiving unto our God."

ONE RULE

"I allow no other rule, whether of faith or practice, than the Holy Scriptures."

"Thus you nullify the word of God by your tradition that you have handed down."

MARK 7:13 NIV

DID YOU KNOW?

Ironically, although the great majority of Wesley's followers were poor, it was simple commoners who persecuted him most.

 THE EGG MAN

One man had filled his pockets with rotten eggs to throw at the preacher. A young man who saw what mischief was intended went behind him, clapped his hands on his pockets, and mashed the eggs all at once. Wesley said: "In an instant he was perfume all over, though it was not so sweet as balsam."

⌒ CONVERTS ⌒ IN CONFLICT

"No sooner do any of them begin to taste of true liberty, but they are buffeted both within and without. The messengers of Satan close them in on every side. Many are already turned out of doors by their parents or masters; many more expect it every day. But they count all these things dung and dross, that they may win Christ."

DID YOU KNOW?

When John and Charles founded the "Holy Club"
as young students at Oxford, not more than five or
six members of the House of Commons went to church.
Later, however, he publicly urged the British colonies
to fully submit to the British king.

⌒ HIS PLACE IN HISTORY ⌒

British society in Wesley's time was in a state of spiritual decline, poverty, and moral degradation. Many claim the revival he helped foster prevented the chaos and anarchy of the French Revolution from occurring in England.

⌒ POWER OVER ⌒
THE ENEMY

"The prince of this world, who knows whereof we are made, will not fail to improve the occasion to disturb, though he cannot pollute the heart which God has cleansed from all unrighteousness."

REDEEMING THE TIME

Being forced to wait, John Wesley exclaimed, "I have lost ten minutes forever!"

A person responded, "Mr. Wesley, you need not be in a hurry."

Replied Mr. Wesley, "A hurry! No; I have no time to be in a hurry. Leisure and I have taken leave of each other."

"The lowest and worst have a claim to our courtesy."

CHARITABLE TO ALL

"There is neither Jew nor Greek, there is neither bond nor free, there is neither male nor female: for ye are all one in Christ Jesus."

GALATIANS 3:28

SIMPLICITY IN CHRIST

"A Scripture Christian I take to be simple in quite another sense than you do: to be quite transparent, far from all windings, turnings, and foldings of behaviour."

⌒ GRADUAL ⌒ SANCTIFICATION

"From the time of our being "born again" the gradual work of sanctification takes place. We are enabled *by the Spirit* to *mortify the deeds of the body*, of our evil nature, and as we are more and more dead to sin, we are more and more alive to God."

GOD MAKES US HOLY

"What God hath promised, he is *able* to perform. Admitting, therefore, that *with men it is impossible to bring a clean thing out of an unclean* — to purify the heart from all sin and to fill it with all holiness — yet *with God all things are possible.*"

⌒ THE IMPORTANCE ⌒ OF THE SACRAMENT

"*Do this in remembrance of me* — by which, as the apostles were obliged to bless, break, and give the bread to all that joined with them in these holy things, so were all Christians obliged to receive these signs of Christ's body and blood."

HOLY COMMUNION

"Here, therefore, the bread and wine are commanded to be received in remembrance of his death, to the end of the world. Observe, too, that this command was given by our Lord when he was just laying down his life for our sakes. They are, therefore, as it were, his dying words to all his followers."

DID YOU KNOW?

John Wesley was not only a preacher, but also served as professor or "fellow" at Lincoln College, Oxford University. His emphasis on methodical holiness came from two classics — William Law's *Serious Call to a Devout and Holy Life,* and Thomas a' Kempis' *Imitation of Christ* — still popular today.

DID YOU KNOW?

John Wesley wrote some 2,600 letters. Two decades before his death his works were published in 32 volumes. His journals spanned approximately 55 years and were published in a 21-part series.

EVERYTHING FOR YOUR GOOD

"God is love, and Christ has died!
That means: the Father himself loves you!
You are his child!
God will not withhold from you
anything that is for your good."

~ GIVING OURSELVES ~
TO GOD

"I...felt a fixed intention to give myself to God. In this I longed to give God all my heart. This is just what I mean by perfection now. I sought after it from that hour."

REAL CHRISTIANITY

"Good sense (so called) is but a poor, dim shadow of what Christians call faith. Good nature is only a faint, distant resemblance of Christian charity. And good manners...is but a dead picture of that holiness of conversation which is the image of God visibly expressed."

UTTER DEPENDENCE

"[Rely] simply on Him that loves you, and whom you love; just as a little helpless child. Christ is yours, all yours: that is enough. Lean your whole soul upon Him!"

"Trust in the Lord with all thine heart; and lean not unto thine own understanding."

PROVERBS 3:5

THE MOST IMPORTANT CHOICE IN LIFE

"Eternal bliss or pain! Everlasting happiness or everlasting misery! One would think it would swallow up every other thought in every reasonable creature."

⌒ THE DAY OF ⌒ THE LORD IS HERE

"Behold, the day of the Lord is come. He is again visiting and redeeming his people. Having eyes, see ye not? Having ears, do ye not hear, neither understand with your hearts? Already his standard is set up. His Spirit is poured forth on the outcasts of men and his love shed abroad in their hearts."

OH FOR A THOUSAND TONGUES TO SING (vv. 1,2)

"Oh for a thousand tongues to sing
My great Redeemer's praise;
The glories of my God and King,
The triumphs of his grace.

"My gracious Master and my God,
Assist me to proclaim,
To spread through all the earth abroad
The honors of thy name.

"Jesus! the name that charms our fears,
That bids our sorrows cease;
'Tis music in the sinner's ears,
'Tis life, and health, and peace.

"He breaks the power of canceled sin,
He sets the prisoner free;
His blood can make the foulest clean;
His blood availed for me."

Charles Wesley

⮞ MY SOUL PROCLAIMS ⮜
THE GREATNESS OF THE LORD

"He [a Christian] is therefore happy in God, yea always happy, as having in him a well of water springing up into everlasting life, and overflowing his soul with peace and joy.

IT ALL BELONGS TO GOD

"The Possessor of heaven and earth placed you here, not as a proprietor, but as a steward."

"The heavens are thine, the earth also is thine."

PSALM 89:11

DID YOU KNOW?

Though he was not a doctor of medicine,
John Wesley found cures for some of the diseases
he had, wrote a book on medicinal cures for the
masses, and started clinics for the poor.

⌒ LOVE GOVERNS ⌒ EVERYTHING

"All is contained in humble, gentle, patient love...
Every right temper, and then all right words and
actions, naturally branch out of love."

~ THE GREAT ~ ETERNAL CHOICE

"How foolish — even mad — it is for one with understanding to prefer deliberately temporal things to eternal. How contrary to all reason to prefer the happiness of a year to the happiness of eternity, for there cannot be any medium between everlasting joy and everlasting pain."

A WOMAN'S DELIVERANCE

"We were desired to call upon a young woman who was in the agonies of despair...almost as soon as we began praying for her, the enemy was cast out, and she was filled with peace and joy in believing."

DID YOU KNOW?

For all the power of his eyes and voice,
John Wesley measured five-feet-three inches tall
and weighed 128 pounds.

"For the Lord seeth not as man seeth;
for man looketh on the outward appearance,
but the Lord looketh on the heart."
1 SAMUEL 16:7

THE GREATEST LOVER

"This all-powerful, all-wise, all-gracious Being, this Governor of all, loves *me*. This lover of my soul is always with me, is never absent; no, not for a moment."

ALL MY HEART

"Go to Christ and tell him, 'Lord Jesus, if you will receive me into your house, if you will but own me as your Servant, ...I will be no longer my own, but give up myself to your will in all things.'"

"I had rather be a doorkeeper in the house of my God, than to dwell in the tents of wickedness."

PSALM 84:10

WE BELONG TO GOD

"[We should have]...thorough conviction that we are not our own; that we are not the proprietors of ourselves, ...a solemn resolution...not to live to ourselves; not to pursue our own desires; not to please ourselves."

⮾ RULES FOR ⮾
CHRISTIAN BEHAVIOR

"1. To use absolute openness and unreserve, with all I should converse with.

2. To speak no word which does not tend to the glory of God; in particular, not to talk of worldly things.

3. To take no pleasure which does not tend to the glory of God; thanking God every moment for all I do take."

⌒ YOUTHFUL AT SIXTY ⌒

At sixty years old, Wesley looked younger, his hair was still dark, and he was in the best physical condition. With renewed vigor he was determined "to reform the nation, and in particular the Church; to spread scriptural holiness over the land."

~ FATHER'S LAST ~ WORDS TO CHARLES

As he lay dying, the father of John and Charles Wesley laid his hands on Charles' head and spoke this prophecy: "Be steady," he murmured. "The Christian faith will surely revive in this kingdom. You shall see it, though I shall not."

FATHER'S LAST WORDS TO JOHN

"The inward witness, son, the inward witness, that is the proof, the strongest proof of Christianity."

"The spirit of man is the candle of the Lord, searching all the inward parts of the belly."

PROVERBS 20:27

⟨ JOHN DESCRIBES ⟩
HIS MOTHER'S LAST
MOMENTS ON EARTH

"She was unable to speak, but I believe quite sensible. Her look was calm and serene, and her eyes fixed upward while we commended her soul to God...'Children, as soon as I am released, sing a psalm of praise to God.' ...It was one of the most solemn assemblies I ever saw or expect to see on this side of eternity."

⟨ JOHN HAS ⟩
NO FEAR OF DEATH

"I shall die into the arms of God. And then farewell sin and pain, then it only remains that I should live with him forever."

WESLEY'S ASSISTANT, JOHN FLETCHER, SAID OF WESLEY:

"Though oppressed with the weight of nearly seventy years, and the care of nearly thirty thousand souls, he shamed still by his unabated zeal and immense labours all the young ministers perhaps of Christendom.

⌒ FLETCHER ON ⌒ HIS ZEAL FOR SOULS:

"He has generally blown the Gospel trumpet and rode twenty miles before most of the professors who despise his labours have left their downy pillows."

THE ONGOING GOSPEL

"God buries His workmen but carries on His work."

Charles Wesley

⌒ ONE OF WESLEY'S ⌒ CONGREGATION RECALLS HIS DYING WORDS

"We knelt down and truly our hearts were filled with the Divine Presence; the room seemed to be filled with God....After a pause he summoned all his strength and cried out, 'The best of all, God is with us.'"

⁓ FAITH, HOPE, ⁓ AND LOVE

"By the grace of God which goes before us,
accompanies us and follows us, continue steadily
in the work of faith, in the patience of hope,
and the labor of love."

❧ A DEFINITION ❧ OF CHRISTIANITY

"It is holiness and happiness, the image of God impressed on a created spirit; a fountain of peace and love springing up into everlasting life."

DID YOU KNOW?

At John Wesley's death in 1791 his followers numbered approximately 79,000 in England and 40,000 in America. By 1957 there were 40 million of his followers worldwide.

BREATHING LIFE INTO DOCTRINE

Wesley insisted he taught only "the plain old religion of the Church of England." By this, he brought divine life into the soul of a nation. His words will always challenge the Church to live above worldly pursuits and direct their attention toward things eternal.

Additional copies of this book and other
portable book titles from **Honor Books**
are available at your local bookstore:

Dwight L. Moody's Little Instruction Book
Martin Luther's Little Instruction Book
Larry Burkett's Little Instruction Book
God's Little Instruction Book (series)